Sh*t People Google

Weird And Funny Google Searches

M. SIMONSEN

©Acanexus Publishing Ltd, 2015
ISBN 978-82-92944-14-1

Although the author has tried to make the information as accurate as possible at the time of writing, no responsibility for any loss, injury or inconvenience sustained by anyone using the information can be accepted. The mentioning of companies, individuals or services in this book does not represent an endorsement; all normal due diligence should be carried out before entering into any contract.

Google is a trademark of Google Inc. and its use in this book is based on the principles of fair and nominative use. The use of the term "Google" in this book does not imply affiliation with or sponsorship by Google Inc.

First Edition: January 2015
Author: M. Simonsen
Production: Acanexus Publishing Ltd
Illustrations: David Fletcher
Cover: Jana Rade, impact studios

"Do you have any problems, other than that you're unemployed, a moron, and a dork?"

—John McEnroe

WARNING: This book contains profanities, bad language and a considerable amount of politically incorrect statements. If you are of a delicate nature or simply think you may find this offensive, you should consider therapy.

SH*T PEOPLE GOOGLE

Acknowledgments

This book could not possibly have come about without the help and assistance from my long-time friends in the SEO and PPC business, particularly John and David who were able to supply almost endless amounts of data. The biggest thanks, though, must go to all those weirdoes, drunks, madmen, lunatics and junkies with too much time on their hands and nothing better to do than searching for shit online. Without you, this book would have been very boring indeed.

SH*T PEOPLE GOOGLE

Preface

I have long suspected that the world is full of truly weird people, people who share with the rest of us only a basic physical reality, but who otherwise inhabit a different dimension altogether. This belief has grown stronger and stronger over the years. It was, for example, strengthened significantly when Herbalife became a listed company and received a further boost when the Laptop Steering Wheel Desk (you can google it) was made available for sale. Yet it was not until I started doing research for this book that I considered the theory just about proven as a fact.

When you embrace the premise that a certain proportion of the population actually inhabits a reality fundamentally different from us, life to a certain degree becomes more bearable.

A phone call to the support department of any major international company, for example, used to be mental torture. I particularly recall the biweekly phone calls from HSBC's fraud department while I was living in the UK. They invariably followed the same lack of logical structure:

"Hello, this is Jaswinder Windaloo from HSBC's fraud department. I need you to verify some card transactions for me. But first I must take you through our security check. Can

you please confirm the amount of the last transaction on your card?"

"I have three cards with you. For which card do you want the last transaction?"

"I am not at liberty to disclose this information until you have passed the security check by confirming the amount of the last transaction on your card."

"Right, but I can't tell you the amount of the last transaction until you tell me for which card you want the last transaction."

"I am sorry, but you have failed our security checks, and as a precaution we will now be blocking your card."

"Oh, OK. Which card will you be blocking?"

"I am not at liberty to disclose this information until…"

I spent a lot of my time in London lining up at HSBC branches and I cannot but feel that had I at the time embraced the theory that these people were not vicious little shits deliberately trying to make my life hell (which was the theory I was working on at the time), but simply ordinary people who inhabited a dimension, a reality, where those sort of calls made sense, I would never have had to start on the blood pressure medication.

Now, armed with the examples in this book, I feel certain that it can finally be proven that such a dimension exists. I haven't given this alternative reality a name yet as I believe further data is needed in order to find a really suitable denomination, but as a working title I have called it the

"Call Center Dimension" based on the fact that its strange, outwardly humanlike creatures seem oddly attracted to jobs in the tele support industry. And I now look at any call to a large support department as a scientific expedition into this alternative reality. I believe that this book can perhaps be a real breakthrough in Call Center Dimension research and that we; for the lack of a better word, "normal" people, if we join forces, over the next few years may be able to gain much more knowledge about how this wild, strange place works. Such understanding may lead to acceptance and a peaceful coexistence with these non-sapient human beings. If that fails, it may as a last resort provide us normal people enough knowledge to exterminate the Call Center Dimension altogether.

A short word about the sources for this book is probably called for. Some search engines publicize searches, most commonly on "latest searches" pages. Much faith in humankind can be lost by staring at such sites for a few hours. The world's by far most popular search engine, Google, however, does not offer such data. True, Google offers a tool called Google Trends, but this site includes data for only the most popular search terms. Luckily for us, total blind madness has not yet spread among the population so badly that the truly weird searches show up there. That leaves us with a couple of alternative methods of peeking into the weird and scary world of google searches. Google's Dimensions, a part of the Google Adwords program, includes exact search phrases. These are sadly available only to the advertiser themselves, and only for those searches that resulted in an ad click. Larger pay-per-click agencies, however, have access to such data for hundreds or even thousands of clients through their Google MCC accounts. Collaboration with several such companies has provided much valuable data for this book.

A more publicly available source of search data is Google's autocomplete feature. Type in "why is my head" in Google and Google may, based on other people's searches suggest "why is my head swollen," "why is my head not square shaped" and so on. No one outside Google, and possibly also no one inside Google, really seems to know exactly how this autocomplete function works. But the rumor that Google is placing small, fast-typing miniature monkeys inside modern PCs is definitely wrong. I have checked. What is certain is that there is a certain volume requirement for a search phrase to be included in autocomplete. Based on the presumption that idiots, like sheep, tend to flock, this should not be a problem. There clearly are, for example, enough morons out there for searches like "Can I get AIDS from killing a mosquito" and "Who invented Spain" to be included. But the most interesting idiot is, in my experience, an idiot who manages to combine blind stupidity with creativity. These genius idiots fly alone, but often in surprising directions. Some of the most fascinating search phrases in this book, thus, come from other sources than Google's autocomplete.

To facilitate a certain reading flow, I have excluded source references from this book. It is after all a book meant to entertain and not a scientific work. For this reason I also use the verb "to google" in the meaning "to search online" rather than the more precise "to search online on Google." Spelling and grammar have also been corrected and a few minor changes here and there have been made to some of the search terms to make them fit better into this book's format and style.

Finally, "Google" is very much a trademark of Google Inc. and its use in this book is based on the principles of fair and nominative use. The use of the term "Google" in this book does not imply affiliation with or sponsorship by Google Inc. In short, Google Inc. has nothing to do with this book whatsoever. If you represent Google Inc. and are interested in discussing a second edition, though, feel free to call me.

SH*T PEOPLE GOOGLE

Contents

SH*T PEOPLE GOOGLE

1.
Pregnancies and Babies

Do babies grow on trees?

Yes, babies grow on trees in much the same way as money doesn't.

Can babies become pregnant?

I know, logically, that it might sound natural for a little baby to be made from a mommy baby and a daddy baby. But if you're old enough to use Google, you're really old enough to know that that is not exactly how this works.

Can babies fly?

This one has an interesting story. Even though I personally think the sentence looks hilarious, I wasn't originally planning to include it in this book because clearly most people who search for this phrase aren't crazy people thinking babies have hidden wings, but just too lazy to finish off the sentence with "on airplanes." But then I came across the search "flying babies real or internet hoax" and sometime later "levitating babies." I realize "levitating babies" is marginally shorter than "can babies go on airplanes," but no one is that lazy. So: The downside is that there are people in the world stupid enough to, if not believe then at least keep the possibility open, that some babies can float around the room like a helium balloon. The upside is that I got to include one of my favorite searches. Note: The "internet hoax" reference may be related to Flying Henry, a project by photographer Rachel Hulin.

Are some babies born in April?

No. Absolutely not. Simply can't happen. No babies are ever born in April. Everyone knows that.

What use is a baby?

Babies were originally invented to prevent oversleeping in parents, but have also turned out to be a good way of preventing the human race from dying out. Modern research, however, indicate that babies tend to prevent parents from having sex, and thus can also be classified as a contraceptive, with the added benefit of being fully accepted and embraced by the Roman Catholic Church (although empirical data there indicates only a mediocre success rate).

Can babies really cry?

This is one of the more puzzling search phrases we came across. Initially I presumed that there must be some hidden sense in this search, as with "can babies fly" above. But I have looked and looked and I simply cannot find any such hidden sense in this search. The only conclusion is that someone, somewhere out there, thinks that the fact that babies cry is actually an Internet hoax or an urban legend. Let's hope they never have children or they are in for a nasty surprise. Note: My editor suggested that the search probably referred to babies crying in the womb. It still makes little sense to me. Everyone knows babies hold their breath for nine months and would obviously drown if they didn't keep their mouths closed.

Who is the oldest baby in the world?

I don't know. I just don't know.

Are some babies green?

Well, they're not allowed on most airlines for the first few months. And they don't own cars. It's not Greenpeace, I know, but still pretty green.

Can kids learn Russian?

Unlike any other languages in the world, Russian cannot be learned by anyone under the age of 36. Up until then people just keep their mouths shut in Russia.

German babies crazy

The structure of the search seems more a conclusion than a question, which makes sense. All German babies are of course absolutely insane. They don't speak until the age of nine, when during dinner they may suddenly say "Mutter, I knov I have not spooken before, but nov I can hold my tongue no more. Thiz sauerkraut iz not up to de required standard." My editor, who is much better at doing proper research than I am (she knows how to google), tells me the search is most likely related to the case of Linda German, a baby snatcher who pleaded insanity during her court case in the 1990s.

Do babies eat?

No. They live on love and air.

Cannibalistic babies

This is one of those truly creepy search terms. I mean, what the f**k was this guy looking for?

Can babies play curling?

Less creepy, more odd. What sort of a weird conversation was this guy having for this to come up, and for him to go "I really don't know; let me google that."

Babies, how long in oven?

This is a silly search. Everyone knows that will depend on whether the oven is preheated or not.

Was Obama ever a baby?

Just as you think you have heard all the odd conspiracy theories, a search term pops up to indicate there are still some you have missed.

Can my baby drive my car?

People are naturally competitive when it comes to their children's development and worried that their babies are not keeping up. Thus it is no surprise that there are tons of searches out there along the lines of "Can a six-month-old baby sit" and "Can a two-month-old baby hold its head up," moving toward the slightly more worrying "can a toddler fart" and "can my four-month-old feel pain." This driving search, though, takes the question to a whole new level. I guess the only way to find out is to strap the little fellow in and hand him the keys.

What if children book?

The answer to that question will depend on what your children book and how old they are. If your child is 25 and he books an around-the-world cruise in your name, you can expect a very nice Christmas present. If, on the other hand, your kid is four and he accidentally books 1,745 tickets for the San Francisco Walking Tours while playing on your iPad, you can expect a pretty nasty credit card bill and some angry emails from some rather surprised tour guides. Then again, if you are looking for what-if children's books, you'd better learn to spell and punctuate before searching online.

Are rich babies worth more?

Figuratively speaking, yes. Per pound on the open market, no.

Why are babies' feet so small?

Because otherwise baby shoes wouldn't fit.

My baby can't read

This is a warning sign, obviously, indicating that there may be something wrong. Mostly with the parents searching for this on Google.

Twins always related

Luckily this is worded as a conclusion, not a question. I presume that whoever searched for this just wanted to inform Google, in case they'd missed this fact.

Why are babies always sticky?

Because parents deliberately cover them in glue.

Washing machine for baby

This is obviously one of those "too lazy to complete the sentence" searches. Because adding the word "clothes" simply takes forever. Or at least that is what we hope it is. To be honest, based on some of the search terms we have seen, you really never know.

Do babies float?

I am going to presume that someone has heard that newborn babies can swim. And then drew his own conclusion to how this could be. Or it could be related to the Floating Henry project. (See "Can babies fly?")

Can you become pregnant from oral sex?

Yes. That is how babies are made.

Can you become pregnant from being fingered?

Oh, I was wrong earlier; this is how babies are made.

Can you become pregnant from a toilet seat?

Um, OK. Maybe that is how babies are made then.

Can you get pregnant from a finger in your ear?

That is not how babies are made. I am pretty confident on this one.

Can you get pregnant from hugging?

Well, it is cozier than a toilet seat, at least.

Will I get pregnant if my dog ejaculated on me?

That is definitely not how babies are normally made, except in some very remote areas.

Can you get pregnant from eating out?

This one really had me puzzled. I mean, how shitty would the restaurant hygiene have to be for you to even begin to worry about this. But then a colleague was kind enough to educate me on current youth slang, and it made more sense. Well, at least it made less not sense.

Can you get pregnant from bathing in sperm?

Let's just say there are easier ways to get pregnant.

Can you get pregnant from not having intercourse?

The search "can you get pregnant without having intercourse" could sort of make sense. And I am going to presume that is what this person meant. But it should be stressed that of all the activities known to man, "not having intercourse" is probably the one least likely to lead to pregnancy.

Why am I not pregnant in India?

This is a tricky one to answer. Could be because you missed the plane? Or because you haven't had sex for years. Or a combination of both. To be honest, I think the range of possible answers to that is simply too great even for Google to be able to help you.

Can a man eat eggs while pregnant?

No. No, he can't.

SH*T PEOPLE GOOGLE

2.
The World

Why are all Chinese good at Ping-Pong?

At this point I would again like to stress the dangers of wild generalizations tending toward racism. To answer the question, though, it is because their eyes make it possible to see the wider picture…

Who invented Spain in the 8th century?

Spain was invented by Mr. John Spain in the year 765. At the time he was trying to invent Norway, but he accidentally put in too much sun.

Why are Spaniards always fat?

Disregarding the prejudice apparent in this question, 14.9% of the adult Spanish population is obese. That leaves 85.1% that aren't fat. Yet we didn't find any records of the search phrase "why aren't Spaniards always fat."

Why did the Spanish try to kill everyone with the flu?

A little knowledge is dangerous, at least in a small mind.

Is Spanish like Italian only different?

Yes. So is English.

Is Spanish like cycling?

This is a tricky one. Unlike a bicycle, Spanish doesn't have wheels, but like cycling you may be exhausted if you do a lot of Spanish while going uphill, at least if you aren't very fit. And like bicycling, being hit by a car while doing Spanish is very dangerous. But unlike bicycles, Spanish doesn't offer a full-body cardio workout. Then again, like cycling, if you learn Spanish once, you are unlikely ever to forget it.

Spaniards are always late

Someone sounds a bit bitter to me. But I guess if you are sitting in a waiting room in Barcelona, waiting for a meeting that should have started two hours ago, and you have free WIFI access, you might just want to check if Google can offer a reasonable explanation.

Why do so many Spanish people speak Mexican?

The Spanish are very good at learning foreign languages. absolutely famed for it. Most Spaniards, from a very early age, will speak languages as different as Mexican, Venezuelan, Peruvian, Bolivian and Argentinean.

Was Jesus from Spain?

See "Why did Jesus take a Latino name."

Is bullfighting an Internet hoax?

How untrusting would you have to be to google this?

London capital Spain

Let's just hope this was someone trying to plan a flight from London and temporarily forgot the name, "Madrid."

Spain is the size of what food?

Well I, uh..it, um, I... No, I have nothing really.

Is Spain in Europe?

Not really funny, just a bit sad.

Is Spain really a ghost?

It is difficult to imagine exactly how much most have gone wrong in a geography class for the student to be left with this question.

Why can't French people fly?

You are wrong in your presumptions. The French, in fact all of France, is an Internet hoax. As we all know, a good hoax can fly around the world in a few hours.

Why are Belgians evil?

People have one bad experience with a Belgian ex-girlfriend and just jump to generalizations like this.

Are there black Russians?

Only with cherries on top.

Are there Swedish fish in Sweden?

Before the Internet, a question like this could drive you mad. Calls to the nearest Swedish consulate and possibly a trip to a Stockholm supermarket disguised as an odd family holiday would have ensued. Today Google can easily inform us that the candy "Swedish Fish" was developed by the Swedish candy producer

Malaco, and yes, they do have them in Sweden though under a different brand ("Swedish Fish" somehow seems less exotic if you are actually in Sweden). Such an increase in efficiency means that the average US idiot can now answer up to 19 times more stupid questions per day than in 1991.

If by "Swedish fish" you meant actual fish, swimming in the ocean, carrying a Swedish passport and/or national ID, however, the answer is "no."

Why do Norwegians look Asian?

Because, like every American knows, Norway is the capital of Asia.

Do Norwegians drink?

No, they simply scrape ice off their beards and eat that to keep themselves hydrated.

Can Germans and Norwegian live together?

The question is weird but what really puzzles me is how come someone felt the need to look this up on the Internet? What sort of strange family reunion was someone planning to feel the need to check if Germans and Norwegians are the human equivalent of antimatter and matter?

Polish people don't like red

This one isn't worded as a question, so probably someone just felt the need to tell Google that people of Polish nationality don't like red or maybe all those manicurists out there are just sick of red nail polish."

Why are some Chinese people from the US?

Ah! Finally we move into a more serious philosophical discussion.

How come some Chinese people are fat?

Science has long been trying to solve this one. So far the most accepted theory is that "they eat too much". Incidentally this would also be why some non-Chinese people are fat.

Do they have phones in China?

No. As we all know, all Asian people talk really loudly and thus need no phones to communicate.

Is it OK to cheat if you're French?

I believe "cheating" is roughly defined as doing something that is not OK. So yes, cheating is OK in France. Sex outside marriage, though, is definitely out.

Is it Christmas in France?

This search would only make sense for about 6 hours every year if, on the 24th of December, you are unsure about the time difference and you wonder if Christmas has started yet in France. Sadly, this search term was found in a Google Adwords campaign in May.

Is Belgium in France?

Yes, Belgium is the former capital of France. It was replaced as capital in 2004 when a famous member of the Hilton family built a new city on the banks of the river Seine, themed on French movies. She named it Nicky after herself.

Are there female Germans?

Speaking from personal experience, no, not in the normal sense of the word. A female in Germany is usually referred to as "an immigrant." See any Wagner opera for further details.

Did the Chinese invent everything?

Yes! Absolutely everything was invented by the Chinese. Except British stiff upper lips which are only manufactured in China on a license from the British Stiff Upper Lip Corporation and sold mainly to graduate students from expensive private schools.

Are there dwarfs in Japan?

Yes. You just don't notice them because they are, in fact, the same height as the rest of the population.

Does the color pink exist in Vietnam?

Only by accident, when white underwear is washed together with brand new red beach towels.

Can French and Germans be friends?

Why should they?

Why do Argentinians think they are white?

I am not sure if the best answer is "do they?" or "because of their skin color."

How come Canadians can't vote?

Because they only vote for a new queen when the old one dies.

Why are there no tigers in Alaska?

Because they got cold feet.

Why is Iceland above water?

Because ice, as we all know, is lighter than water and thus floats.

Why are Americans retarded?

To make Canadians look smarter than they really are.

Do Americans bounce?

Not entirely sure what this person was trying to find on the Internet. But to answer the question seriously: It's a bit of a balancing act. Drop them from too low and they simply walk away, drop them from too high and they just go "splat." Getting an American to bounce requires just the right drop.

Why do Floridians live longer?

Life expectancy in Florida is about average for the US. In fact in 2012 it ranked only 22 out of all US states. Presumably this guy just saw a lot of movies from Miami with old people and reached a logical and completely wrong conclusion.

Why do Floridians dress?

This is one of those WTF questions. "Because otherwise they'd be naked" is as good an answer as I can come up with.

Why is blue hair common in Florida?

The "blue hair gene" is indeed commonly found in Florida. Research in genetic mobility, origin and evolution indicates that it was brought to Florida in the late 16th century by a little old lady called Bertha.

How can you stop someone from Texas?

A "free if you can eat it 72oz. steak" sign along the road can apparently succeed where the United States Supreme Court and Mexican armies failed.

Does New Jersey exist?

No. It's a fictional place invented by Hollywood. This is why you have never actually, in real life, met anyone from Trenton.

Should I be afraid of people from Idaho?

Hell, yes. Be very, very afraid. Anyone who's willing to wear rubber waders is mentally unstable.

Is it illegal to urinate in the UK?

Owing to frequent flood problems, the UK enacted the Urination and Taking the Piss (England) Act 2009 (the Piss Act). Under this new law, within the borders of England, you are only allowed to urinate up to the same amount (measured by volume) as you have actually drunk during your stay there. It is thus extremely important to keep all receipts for any drink you buy. This has led to a significant increase of day tourists to Wales and explains why public toilets in the Cardiff area are often out of service.

Is Helsinki or Stockholm closer to the equator?

These are two of the most northern capitals in the world. Why on earth would you word your question like that? It's like asking "what is safer, a nuclear bomb or the plague?"

3.
Religion

Does God ever speak through cats?

Hey! Freaky, old cat lady in the run-down, scary villa down the road finally got broadband.

Buddhism was born inside a cat

This is another statement, rather than a question. Even Google is clearly baffled by this though, and the best it can do is suggest a Wikipedia article about Cat Stevens.

Did Jesus get stoned or drunk?

Oh, dear. I heard that early Christians got stoned, or I think I heard it, or maybe they weren't stoned, just drunk, I am not sure really… To be honest I am rather confused.

Did Jesus smoke pot?

Key in "did Jesus smoke" in Google and you will get a range of interesting searches. I am not sure what version of the Bible is being published these days, but clearly the King James Bible is not the standard in some circles.

Why did Jesus take a Latino name?

"Hesus" Christ!

What does God really think of me?

This may be a very interesting question. But why would anyone look for the answer in Google? Everyone knows God is on Twitter these days.

Did Jesus ever joke around?

Just glancing at this, you might think "OK, fair enough question." But let's be honest: Who would want to know? How insecure about your religious preferences would you have to be to think, "OK, he died for our sins, I can buy that, but what I really need to know to commit to this religion is 'Is he a fun guy'?" You wouldn't want to go to heaven and find it a dull place.

Can Buddhists really fly?

Yes, but not if they are more than seven months pregnant.

Where does God hide on a clear day?

I love this search. It shows a lateral thinking in a small, weird mind. The answer, of course, is that God isn't hiding; he is just sky colored.

Can Buddhists be religious?

And can birds fly? That is an actual search too, or at least "can birds fly in the rain" which is as close as this to make no difference.

How to become a saint quickly?

To die is a good start. Oh, and try to be nice.

What is more expensive: gold or religion?

Per pound, religion is definitely more expensive.

Is God big in Israel?

This one clearly must have followed the sentence "Hi, excuse me, my spacecraft just crashed on this planet."

4.
Illness And Health

Why can't I look at myself in the mirror?

Because you're a vampire?

Down syndrome vaccination

OK. I know this is probably someone searching for information about vaccinations for their kid with Down syndrome. But then again, my experience from putting this book together means that we can also safely presume that some people out there thinks Down Syndrome is contagious and worry that their kids might catch Down Syndrome in kindergarten. Let me reassure you: If you're that stupid and you have kids, a bit of Down Syndrome won't make a difference.

My editor, who knows everything, points out that the search may also be related to Jenny McCarthy and her anti-vaccine movement. Since Down syndrome is determined in utero, before the possibility of vaccination, of the child at least, it doesn't really make the search any less sad.

Part-time job as Down syndrome

A slightly more insane variation of a similar search term we found: "Down syndrome vacancies." Because basically Down Syndrome is a pretty cool job.

Is being tall an illness?

Only if you're short and bitter.

Why does my belly button smell?

The answer depends on how it smells. If you think it smells like chocolate it could be because you have been playing some naughty sex games recently (or just lost a piece of chocolate down there when you were gorging on candy in bed last night). If you think it smells like lavender and roses, it may be due to perfume. If you think it smells just plain bad, you probably should shower more often. And if you think it smells like freshly ground coffee from a Parisian corner café, warm croissants and early spring morning air, you probably should have your head examined.

Can I get sick from drinking after my cat

OK, cat lady is online again. I don't know what you're drinking after your cat, but if it is from the same cup or saucer you're already sick.

Can I become sick from thinking the same thing twice?

This is definitely a candidate for the top position in the WTF category. I really don't know what else to say.

How to become sick

Boy, did we find many odd variations on this search: "how to become sick," "how to become sicker," "how to become really ill" and so on. What is wrong with you people?

Become sick by thinking hard about it

It is already sick to think about thinking hard about being sick so that you can become sick. So yes, it worked.

Can you get AIDS from fighting too much?

Not if you take precautions and wear a condom.

Can you get AIDS from killing a mosquito?

Only if you f**k it to death.

Can you get AIDS from rusty metal?

Sure. That is how AIDS started. The HIV virus, as is now well documented, lives in old metal and rotten wood and sneaks out at night looking for someone to bite.

Is coughing with pneumonia good

In general I would say that it is as good as not coughing with pneumonia. On the whole I think, though, that anything with "pneumonia" is not going to fall into the category "really great."

Is pneumonia better than pleurisy?

Why, oh why, would you look this up? I mean it is not like the doctor is going to give you a choice: "Yeah, you're clearly very sick. Would you prefer pneumonia or pleurisy?" Also, considering that pleurisy is most commonly caused by pneumonia, I think in general it can be presumed not to be a whole lot better.

Red face causes alcoholism

Right. Someone clearly missed a lecture on cause and effect.

Alcoholics are Russian

That is very true. Indeed one of the saddest facts of being an alcoholic is that it also means you have a one in seven chance of being Russian.

Good luck breaking a leg

Thank you, that is very kind of you.

Can you survive without a head?

Before I started this book, I would have said this was a pretty obvious question to answer. Now, though, I am not so sure.

Can you get sick from licking a toilet?

There is a story behind this question; I am sure of it. And I don't want to know it.

Can you get sick from licking a live chicken?

I am going to presume that this is asked not entirely as a theoretical question. And thus sadly we must conclude that someone, somewhere, decided to lick a live chicken and then thought "Gee, I wonder if that was really a smart thing to do."

Is a nail through the foot painful?

They say experience is the teacher of fools. So please, please try this yourself.

What are lungs for?

Surely everyone knows they are mostly for contracting pneumonia, COPD and cancer and causing a painful death.

Is being dead like being born but different?

Yes.

Do hypochondriacs ever get sick?

No. They are immune.

Can you cure a hypochondriac by making him ill?

Of all the searches I found during the research for this book, this is probably my absolute favorite. They say that there is a thin line between being a genius and being crazy, and I think this one balances just in the middle. The logic is infallible. As hypochondriasis is normally defined as "an unwarranted fear that one has a serious disease," of course you can technically cure people of hypochondria by making the fear "warranted," for example, by giving them a serious disease. Since the fear is no longer unwarranted, the person no longer meets the criteria for hypochondriasis and thus the person has, de facto, been cured. This is wonderful lateral thinking from a person who definitely needs to be banned from ever practicing medicine.

What is a fever on the Kelvin scale?

If someone sold you a Kelvin scale body thermometer, you really need to change your pharmacy.

Why can't I look after myself?

Because you spend too much time googling shit.

Why can't I wear a tampon?

Because you're a man?

Why can't I sit down and study?

Because someone stole your chair?

Why do I have a nail in my head?

We found no searches for "how to get a nail out of my head." Someone seriously needs to reevaluate priorities. Curiosity killed the cat.

Are there gay bacteria?

During what for the lack of a better word we will refer to as "the research" for this book, we found endless searches along the lines of "Are there gay cats," "Can mice be gay" and so on. Interesting questions, of course, but none of them really seemed entertaining enough to make the cut. That is, until we found this one. Of course this sentence can have a number of meanings. If someone says "those shoes are really gay," she is probably not making a statement about the sexual preferences of the footwear in question, but using the word rather in its modern, colloquial sense, meaning basically uncool. "Are there unhip bacteria" would ipso facto, however, also infer that the person has already established that there definitely are fashion-oriented bacteria. On the other hand, if the user was an older one, say 150 years or so, he or she might have been using the word in the rather opposite meaning of "fun." "Are there fun bacteria?" he or she might have asked, looking for some sort of hilarious illness to contract. Then again it could be that someone heard that there are in fact gay cats and dogs and wanted to find out how far down the evolutionary scale ass bandits are found. We may never know the truth. Note: If you have ever googled "are there gay bacteria" and would like to be featured in a future edition of this book, please send more information about your search together with a headshot to help@imamoronreallyiam.iq. Mark your email "What was I thinking?"

How big are my ears?

Of course this would be a tricky one for any search engine to answer. A mirror would be my preferred source of more information. But in general, since you are actually googling this, my guess would be "pretty big."

5.
Animals

Rabbits are evil

Another one of those "there is a story in there somewhere" search phrases. And this one has to be good.

Can dogs really die?

I know there is quite some competition for the top spot on the WTF list, but this one I really feel has a good chance.

What to do if kangaroos attack?

The answer, apparently, is "walk away sideways." The walking away part seems to make sense. Exactly why you have to do it sideways is a little more uncertain. Slate.com also informs us that "Special instructions apply if the attacking kangaroo is a male displaying dominance behavior." Worth keeping in mind.

Can dogs see faces?

No, definitely not. Dog cannot see live faces, but can apparently see faces if displayed on TV screens.

Do dogs have brains?

No. Dogs are classified as subphylum Crustacea, along with lobsters and crabs, and have an extensive fossil record dating back as far as the Cambrian period, 543 million years ago. Most dogs today are free-living aquatic animals with a segmented body, a chitinous hard exoskeleton and paired, jointed limbs. They have only limited central nervous systems comprised primarily of a suboesophageal ganglion, thoracic ganglia and a ventral nerve cord. No wait, I'm thinking of shrimps.

Can I fingerprint my neighbor's dog

First of all I would like to thank you for including the word "print" in that search. As for the question itself, I am afraid only the police are allowed to fingerprint your neighbor's dog, provided the dog is believed on reasonable grounds to have committed, been charged with, or summonsed to answer a charge for, an indictable offence or summary offence referred to in Amendment 26 of the Declaration of Independence.

Are cats green or blue?

Yes. Yes, they are.

Help a cat eat my rabbit

Google is perhaps not the best place to request assistance of this type. Simply grab a knife and cut the rabbit into smaller pieces and the cat should manage fine.

Why do birds attack aircrafts?

This is a common misunderstanding. Only really big birds attack aircrafts on purpose. Before they fly out on their last mission these birds will drink sake and put on a white headband with white circle.

Can birds be pregnant?

Birds reproduce by cell division. Well-known fact.

Can birds smell farts?

Oh dear, a little Polly Parrot is suffering something dreadfully somewhere.

Do birds get eaten?

Only by accidents and deliberately.

What would happen if I glued a cat's paws to my ceiling?

You would turn its world upside down.

Are all rabbits in movies dead?

And the WTF list just got longer.

Rabbits are not chickens

Thankfully this is not worded as a question. Someone simply found it necessary to inform Google.

Can cats breathe underwater?

Yes! That is why newborn kittens are sometimes put in a sack and thrown in the river. It helps them breathe.

Do rats lay eggs?

I thought this one was weird until I saw the next one.

Can rats lay eggs in my brain at night?

Someone is having some really nasty nightmares.

Why must I let sleeping dogs lie?

It's more of a polite request really.

All things equal a rabbit

Now, that isn't entirely true, though, is it?

Can squirrel blood cure warts?

I definitely missed the Myth Busters episode on this one.

Is that a cat?

Top search result in Google is a Wikipedia article on "cat communication," which apparently is "the transfer of information by one or more cats that has an effect on the current or future behavior of another animal, including humans. Cats use a range of communication modalities including vocal, visual, tactile and olfactory." Not really an answer to the question, but it does illustrate well how much shit is out there if you are willing to dig deep enough.

6.
Books and
Movies

Did Charlie Chaplin ever meet Napoleon?

Two funny little men, both at one point shooting in France. Of course they met.

Is Harry Potter real?

Unlike the TV series The Kennedys, which is entirely made up, the Harry Potter movies – and books – are indeed based on true events.

Is Dora the Explorer based on a true story?

Yes. The animated TV series about the seven-year-old Latina girl who embarks on quests to faraway places accompanied by her talking purple backpack and anthropomorphic monkey companion named Boots is indeed based on real events and real people.

Can Harry Potter fly first class?

Another one for the WTF list.

Can some books walk?

And here is a companion.

If I have a book, what do I have?

OK. Someone just discovered those square things with a lot of pages with writing on them.

What is my favorite book?

A seemingly sensible question, until you realized someone just asked it of Google. How confused and insecure would you have to be to google what your own favorite book is? And how on earth would Google know.

Is it dangerous to burn books?

Well, in fact yes. Didn't turn out too good for the Nazis.

Can books conduct electricity?

The real interesting question is, of course, really what sort of weird situation the person googling this must have been in. How bad must your relationship with your local electrician be for you to end up trying to fix your own electrical circuit with books.

Books based on movies

I honestly just read past this when I saw it on a query list and then about 10 seconds later my brain went "Wait a minute. That is the wrong way around, isn't it?" Then obviously I laughed a lot...until I learned that there are quite a number of books based on movies. How sad.

Did Shakespeare make any movies?

Yes, but because this is like a really, really long time ago, they were all black and white movies.

Did Shakespeare smoke crack?

Why would you search for this? I mean, seriously, even if you think some of his plays and sonnets are perhaps a bit tricky to understand, why would your first thought be, not "This must be a really old text," but "Shit, man, dude's on crack." And then what made you take the step from thinking this to actually googling to see if you were right?

Is Shakespeare based on a real person?

Yes. The character of Shakespeare is based on Mr. Oswald Ingram Buckley of 9 You've Got To be Kidding Me Avenue, New York, New York. The only slight difference is that Mr. Buckley never published any texts, was an accountant without much imagination and died in 1938. The rest is pretty much the same.

Did Shakespeare live before he died?

"Jane, could you bring out the WTF list again? Yes, I think we have another one."

What was Henrik Ibsen named?

"To be honest, Jane, it is probably easier if you just leave it on my desk."

If I have two movies, can I watch them?

Someone actually asked Google this. Google's best suggestion was "Watch Out! Family Movies that Could Traumatize Your Kids" from a site called www. commonsensemedia.org.

Why are old movies not all black and white?

Because they trained monkeys to color in the images in 1984.

Can you write a book about something that didn't happen?

No. Absolutely not. There is a law against that: the Stephen King's Act of 1784.

Am I allowed to write an autobiography?

Sadly yes. There should be a law against that, though. Chelsea Handler has written five of them and that is definitely at least five too many.

Are books better than Plasma TVs?

I love how specific this search is. Someone had heard that reading the book is supposed to be better than watching the movie, but then he got a new wide-screen plasma and just wanted to make absolutely sure.

What is the name of someone who writes plays?

I don't think there is a title for that job. You can just make something up. Like "playwriter", or "playwrite." Weird. Autocorrect keeps changing it to "playwright."

SH*T PEOPLE GOOGLE

7.
Politics

Was Ronald Reagan a woman?

There is clearly no limit to the conspiracy theories out there.

Was Ronald Reagan a horse whisperer?

Seriously, someone searched online for that.

Why didn't Ronald Reagan marry Margaret Thatcher?

What worries me the most is that someone is clearly sufficiently well informed to realize that politically this question make sense, and yet insane enough to google it.

Woman murdered Obama

President Barack Obama has had his ups and downs during his two terms as president, but as far as we can tell, being killed is not one of them. This search was on my WTF list until my editor informed me that this search most likely is related to the myth that a woman was killed for knowing where Obama was born.

George Bush named after airport?

This is a common misunderstanding. George H. W. Bush was not named after George Bush Intercontinental Airport in Houston. He was named after George W. Bush, his son.

8.
School

Can teachers die?

Yes, but you must use a silver bullet and a stake through the heart.

Are teachers more likely to go blind?

Only if you poke them in the eye.

Can teachers afford to live?

No. The average life span of a teacher is 12.5 days, after which time they usually run out of food and water and perish.

Can art teachers have tattoos?

No, their skin simply can't be penetrated by tattoo needles. Snaps the needle in half.

Can teachers have arms?

Please let this question refer to guns.

Why can teachers just teach?

Because the dentists protested when they started pulling out teeth.

Why do we need schools?

To reduce the number of stupid questions on Google.

Why are schools Ivy League?

Don't worry, yours isn't.

Why do I need to learn to spell?

This one was changed for improved readability from "Wy do I need to learn 2 spel." Asked and answered, as they say in the courtroom dramas.

Why is English so perfect?

They say modesty is the virtue of the lukewarm.

How can I learn to count to ten in English?

This is obviously a sensible search. Anyone learning English may, early on in his or her studies, want to learn this. What I really want to know is how someone can actually write, in perfect English, "How can I learn to count to ten in English" without actually knowing how to count to ten in English. I would definitely ask for my money back after that English course.

SH*T PEOPLE GOOGLE

9.
Just Plain Stupid

How to go to the toilet?

Toddlers today, hey? They learn to google even before potty training.

Why is snow so cold?

To cool down the polar bears.

Which farts smell the worst?

Yes, that is right. Someone googled that. My editor, who knows more than any person should have to know, tells me that vegetarians' farts would be on top of the list.

How to boil ice?

Very, very quickly is usually recommended. Although in fairness this search does return a few links to some interesting science experiments.

How to know if you're tall?

Oh, this is a tricky one. If you are always the first one to notice that it is raining, though, it's a pretty safe indication that you're tall.

Is it rape if you accidentally fell on her naked?

Oh, that is going to be one short trial.

What is the point of amnesia?

I just can't remember.

What day is Monday?

Tuesday?

What color is red?

Red is basically orange that couldn't afford yellow.

Four triplets

This search makes me curious. Clearly you can have four sets of triplets. Sadly I expect this person wasn't looking for that.

Learn to speak with a lisp

Some people are just born with it; others have to study hard.

How to call a friend?

How to call a friend what?

How long is quite long in meters?

This is another of my personal favorites. Not only is the absurdity of wanting to convert an entirely imprecise term from one precise measurement to another hilarious, but it also gave me hours of fun trying to come up with any situation where a rough estimate in meters, "oh, about three to seven meters I'd say" was required, yet where you absolutely could not use the phrase "oh, quite long I reckon."

Do dwarfs really exist?

Of course not. They are just Japanese people with albinism.

Best Halloween costume made from beer cans

Well, I guess they celebrate Halloween in hick towns too.

Can inflatable dolls work?

Only in a very limited range of jobs. They are generally considered absolutely useless as doctors and criminal lawyers, but some have found successful careers in politics.

Are there hats?

No. They exist only in old films. This search most likely refers to a quote by comedian John Oliver commenting on a recent poll showing that one out of four are skeptical of the effects of climate change, commenting: "You don't need people's opinion on a fact. You might as well have a poll asking: 'Which number is bigger, 15 or 5?' or 'Do owls exist?' or 'Are there hats?' "

Are there jobs in Florida?

No. There are no jobs in Florida. Not a single one. They have all been outsourced to India.

Are there kangaroos in Africa?

The Macropus Giganteus Ignoramus, Giant Large-footed Moron, is the only known kangaroo in Africa. It too was really supposed to live in Australia but it was too stupid to read the memo.

Are there KFCs in Kentucky?

No. The world's second-largest restaurant chain, Kentucky Fried Chicken, does not exist in the state of Kentucky.

Are there laws in Japan?

No. Japan is well known for its tendency toward anarchy.

Is the moon really hollow?

It's the word "really" that I think bothers me the most about this search. It indicates that someone sort of believed it as a fact, but just wanted to double check.

SH*T PEOPLE GOOGLE

10.
Technology and Science

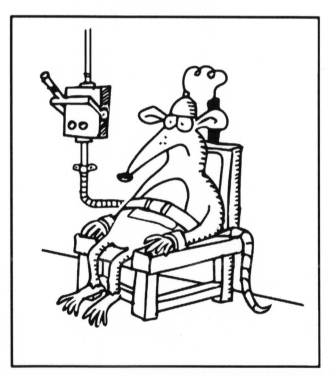

How much electricity to kill a mouse?

A mousetrap is probably easier.

What would happen if I backup my iPhone?

The same data will exist in two places at the same time, thus violating one of the basic laws of nature. The result will be a wormhole into another dimension and eventually the destruction of Earth and the inner parts of the solar system.

How much data do I need for my computer?

For a desktop PC you should have at least five data. For a laptop, four data may be better because data is heavy to carry around.

Can I live without a computer?

If you actually decide that the best way to find the answer to that question is to google it, I reckon the answer is a pretty clear: "Hell no!"

Do I need a TV license for my dog?

And yet another one for the WTF list.

Am I on the Internet now?

Yup. Someone googled that. Even more sadly there is a whole website available to tell you if you're on the Internet or not: www.amiconnectedtotheinternet.com. Clearly I am the only one who sees the logical flaw in that.

How to make a fire with matches?

If people would only read the f'ing manual before asking questions.

How to use a knife?

If you don't know whether to grip the blunt or sharp end, you shouldn't be making your own food.

How to use a chair to lock a door?

1) Find key-shaped chair. 2) Insert into keyhole. 3) Turn clockwise.

How to use a book to hide things?

1) Find a big book. 2) Put in front of things.

How to burn wood?

1) Expose to open flame. 2) Repeat as required.

How to wear sandals?

Sandals, as is well known, are notoriously difficult to put on. It is generally recommended to enlist the help of a professional.

How to shampoo your hair?

Again enlisting professional help is usually recommended unless you have received special training.

How much water is too much?

That depends entirely on the purpose. If you are replicating the Pacific Ocean, 2 million gallons is not enough; if you're planning to boil an egg, it might be overkill.

My editor insists that the person googling this definitely was referring to hyponatremia, a condition where drinking too much water causes the level of salt, or sodium, in your blood to drop too low. I think the person googling this was just an idiot.

Is the moon real?

What moon?

Are there cats on Mars?

No. The "curiosity" referred to in the saying "curiosity killed the cat" is not the NASA Curiosity Mars Rover.

What is absolute zero in kelvin?

On a scale that starts from absolute zero on one end, and has boiling water at 373, absolute zero would be, oh, I don't know, about a million. Yea. Definitely a million or so.

Is irony heavy?

Irony is a mental-like element with the symbol Mrn and atomic number 4980. It's a non-ferrous humor, and quite rare in some parts of the world. It is generally said that Americans lack irony (though said mostly by non-Americans) and America's dependence on imported irony (mostly from Britain which is a net exporter of irony) has been of some concern to many U.S. policymakers.

Are super cars always fast?

Although you probably could make a super slow car, commercially it is unlikely to be a big success. It was tested with the Vector W8, which instead of actually moving, according to some accounts merely set tennis star Andre Agassi's garden on fire, and Aston Martin's Lagonda who's astonishingly unreliable electronic in general made the car just sit very still with its vipers and indicators on.

Why do people always say velocity is a vector quantity and speed is not?

Clearly we don't hang in the same circles.

Why does my car AC smell like pee?

Could be a stopped-up drain line, could be someone pissed in the air vent.

Is it possible to grow taller?

Nope. Six-foot-tall people were born like that.

Can you drink upside down?

We just don't know. During experiments the water kept falling out of the cup.

Can I sleep in a fridge?

On the whole, installing air conditioning is recommended.

What is LinkedIn for?

No one actually seems to really know the answer to that one. It must be something important, though, since so many people are using it.

How to make a survival bracelet?

If you really ended up in a major crisis situation, your airplane crashing on a deserted island, a super volcano erupting or just general end-of-the-world stuff, having access to survival equipment is obviously essential. But on the list of survival stuff to bring, how far down would you have to go before you find "bracelet"? Unless it is way down toward the bottom of a very, very long list – next to survival nail polish – you are probably going to look pretty silly when disaster strikes.

11.
What would
happen if…

What will happen if I connect my iPhone to my brain?

Your iPhone becomes just a little bit dumber.

What would happen if I ate 100,000 calories in a day?

You'd be too fat to google stupid crap.

What would happen if I ate my laptop?

If it was a Windows-based laptop you'd take 20 minutes to get up in the morning, you'd get slower and slower during the day, constantly suffering from virus infections and your evenings would normally end with you crashing suddenly into a blue wall while babbling random hexadecimal numbers before finally falling slowly backward into bed.

What would happen if I ate myself?

Confucius says "Every amateur philosopher should remember that silence is a true friend who never betrays." By the way, there is an online blog where this question is discussed in great length. The two possible answers seem to be "You'll disappear" and "You'll become twice as big." I personally wish they would all try it in practice and stop taking bandwidth that the world requires for more intelligent purposes.

What would happen if I cut off my balls?

You'd regret it. The world wouldn't.

What would happen if I shot myself in the head?

People might ask "Is that a new hairdo?" but otherwise it is unlikely anyone would notice any difference.

What would happen if I ate a blue whale?

Greenpeace would hunt you down and kill you.

What would happen if I cut off my cat's whiskers?

You'd have a silly-looking cat.

What happens if I cut off circulation to a limb?

Nothing beats empirical data so please go ahead and test. Start with your head and keep us updated on the progress.

What would happen if an airplane was on the moon?

It would win the Google Lunar X-PRIZE.

What would happen if you snort AJAX?

You'd get clean sinuses, and then you'd die.

What will happen if I don't eat for a month?

You become so thin that eventually you have a negative mass and turn into a black hole.

What will happen if I eat a banana before bed?

You avoid dreaming that you wish you'd eaten a banana before bed.

What would happen if I eat healthy?

You'd live longer and have more children. Please don't.

What will happen if I walk a mile in another man's shoes?

You'd be a mile away from a guy looking for his shoes. A warning to parents and teachers: Other signs that indicate you may want cut down on your metaphors and similes are finding any type of skeleton in cupboards, observing your kid trying to kill a cat with curiosity or noticing your kid trying to put out a fire with a lighter and a can of gasoline.

What would happen if I cloned myself?

The world would have one more moron.

How can I stop my screen from rotating?

See "How can I get rid of a poltergeist?"

How can I get rid of a poltergeist?

Take your medication. In the unlikely event that this does not solve the issue, there is a website for others with diminished mental capacities called paranormalsoup.com. The advice there states that

"Salt may not help" but also helpfully suggests "Pray to a tree for protection and guidance."

Why are my arms so long?

Because if not, they wouldn't reach up to your armpit. And that would just look silly.

Obsessive compulsive drinking disorder

Nice try, but I think you may find you're just an alcoholic.

SH*T PEOPLE GOOGLE

12.
Food

Who was Al Dente?

Alessandro "Al" Dente, 11th Duke of Lasagna (b. 1542, d. 1611), invented the not completely overcooked pasta. He is today celebrated in Italian restaurants across the world and is the patron saint of dentists.

Is tomato pronounced tomato?

Well as the song goes, "You say tomato and I say tomato." So, no. The correct pronunciation is "tomato."

What are oranges good for?

This is an interesting question. I have tried to use them as billiard balls, but the result was less than satisfactory.

Can you book a table at McDonald's?

And that is why she didn't accept your proposal.

13.
Crime and
Law

Why do police officers eat doughnuts?

Because you can stick them on your arm as a wrist band. Useful if you have to grab for your gun to shoot a baddie while having a snack.

Do you need to rinse and repeat?

Yes. Anything that is written on a bottle of shampoo is considered law in the Western world. Failure to comply with such instructions can result in civil and/or criminal penalties, including imprisonment up to one year, fines of up to $ 500,000 and a very, very bad hair day.

Is everything a crime?

Yes, except stupidity. Clearly that is allowed.

Can I make my own laws?

Yes. The process usually involves starting a political party and winning a majority in whatever legislature your country has. However, WikiHow has an article on how to make your own laws in eight easy steps. They start with "Get a notebook and place the words 'Laws' on the front with a permanent marker. It is important to make the book look as official as possible."

Are all laws about abortion?

Yes. Every single one of them. In all countries, all laws are about abortion.

Are there laws against blackmail?

No. As pointed out before they are all about abortion.

Is it true that nothing is illegal until you get caught?

Why would you get caught if it was legal?

Why are all cops bald?

On the positive side, you clearly have a limited experience with law enforcement. On the negative side, you're a moron.

Are prisons good or bad?

Prisons, like New Jersey hotels, appear much better from the outside.

Can I shoot someone in my apartment?

This depends mostly on three factors: Do you have a gun, do you know how to use it and is there someone in your apartment? If these three factors are present you should be able to shoot someone in your apartment. If one of these factors is missing, say for example that there is someone in your house, you know how to use a gun but you don't have a gun available, shooting someone in your apartment may pose a problem. Be aware that if you do successfully manage to shoot someone in your apartment, you may have to go to jail.

Can you hit a girl?

You can hit on girls. The "on" is important.

Can you hit someone with glasses?

There are two ways to understand this question, so we must provide two different answers. 1) Only if they have red hair and braces. 2) Yes, but your glasses are likely to break.

Can you smash a car window with one finger?

Yes. But really professional car thieves use their heads. This search, by the way, is probably related to an Internet myth based on a Youtube video posted in 2011.

Is it illegal to walk through a drive-through?

No. Just really, really stupid.

Is it illegal to beat someone up?

Not if you see them walking through a drive-through.

How can I steal money without getting caught?

Break into your own house, take your own money and convince yourself not to report the break-in to the police.

Can a chair make a decision?

Possibly someone with a question about company law, possibly someone who is off his rocker.

Can I drive with my permit?

If it is a driver's permit, yes. If it is a parking permit, maybe not so much.

14.
Searches I Just Couldn't Be Bothered To Comment On

Are horses blind?

Can I run every day?

Can you write a letter to a judge?

Why do we say aww?

Why do we say our goodbye?

Can I make a pillow of concrete?

Is there dark light?

What would happen if cats could fly?

Where does Catherine live?

Can I eat rock?

What would happen if I drank milk?

Did NASA invent thunderstorms to cover up space battles?

Can I make a call with an apple?

How can I heat up food without a microwave oven?

How to make a fire with Photoshop?

How to make a fireman?

Where is Europe?

Why does England not have a king?

Can you piss off Siri?

Where does Adam live?

Are there buildings on Mars?

Are there dinosaurs on Mars?

Am I a psycho?

Why does no one like me?

Is it dangerous to hold a metal pole in a thunderstorm?

Why not both?

How can I sell ice to an Eskimo?

Why does my cat always pee on me?

Are there flying spiders?

Can women have it all?

Why do all the parents die in Disney movies?

Why do all the diseases come from Africa?

Why did all the apostles have modern English names?

Why do all the buildings in Paris look the same?

Why can't everyone be rich?

Why do all the countries end in stan?

Why do all the Disney stars go crazy?

Why does everyone with Down Syndrome look the same?

Why do all the fat chicks like me?

Why do the Kardashians begin with 'k'?

Why do all roads lead to Rome when I want to go to Paris?

Why do all movie stars eventually die?

Why do all sandwiches have mayo?

Why do all serial killers go to Portland?

Why does God end relationships?

Why did I buy a Playstation?

Oh, why did I buy a Chevy Silverado?

Is there caffeine in coffee?

What are cars used for?

Why is everything reversed in the UK?

Can the sun be seen from space?

Can the moon just disappear?

And for the grand finale, the Google search for:

How do I use google?

Did you like this book?

Find more similar books on http://acanexus-publishing.com.

Made in the USA
Middletown, DE
04 December 2021

54207169R00061